THE BIG BOOK ON
NATIVE AMERICAN
TRUTHS

Tribes and Their Ways of Life

Children's Geography & Cultures Books

BABY PROFESSOR BOOKS

First Edition, 2019

Published in the United States by Speedy Publishing LLC, 40 E Main Street, Newark, Delaware 19711 USA.

© 2019 Baby Professor Books, an imprint of Speedy Publishing LLC

Baby Professor Books are available at special discounts when purchased in bulk for industrial and sales-promotional use. For details contact our Special Sales Team at Speedy Publishing LLC, 40 E Main Street, Newark, Delaware 19711 USA. Telephone (888) 248-4521 Fax: (210) 519-4043. www.speedybookstore.com

10 9 8 7 6 * 5 4 3 2 1

Print Edition: 9781541968776

Digital Edition: 9781541968851

Hardcover Edition: 9781541968813

See the world in pictures. Build your knowledge in style.
https://www.speedypublishing.com/

CONTENTS

Native Americans were the first inhabitants of North America. They had their own customs and traditions even before the first foreigners arrived on their lands. To this date, much of these customs and traditions remain untouched; and we're going to read about them in this big book on Native American truths. Let's get started!

CHAPTER 1:
What Is A Native American Society Like?

An important role in the traditional Native American societies was their social structure. While there were no written rules or no complex government, they did have a definitive structure as well as social norms and people were expected to follow these roles if they desired to be included in their society.

Native American Society

A TRIBE OR A CLAN?

The tribes, also referred to as nations, were at the highest level. They were big groups of people that had geography, language, and culture in common.

Native American Tribe

Native American Clans

Clans were the smaller groups of people within the tribe. The members of the clan typically shared a common ancestor and were considered to be related to each other. Each clan was represented by its own spirit or symbol that provided the clan with a name. While many of the clans were named from animals, some of them were not. Some examples of clan names are Deer, Bear, Snow, Water and Hawk.

Membership in a clan would be determined in some tribes by the child's mother and in other tribes by the child's father.

Clan Mother

In some of the tribes, the "clan mother" was a woman that was the head of the clan. She did not have any real power, but she was respected by all.

THE CHIEF

Leaders of the tribes and clans were referred to as chiefs. These were men that were chosen or elected by the people. Typically, they didn't have total power, however, they were respected and would provide advice that the tribe or clan would typically follow.

Chief Spotted Elk

Chief Black Hawk

The tribe might have both a war leader as well as a civil leader. The war leader would guide the tribe during times of war, and the civil leader would take over during peaceful times.

Buffalo Bull's Back Fat Head War Chief of the Blood Indians

Dennis Banks, Native American Civil Rights Leader

The shaman, often referred to as the medicine man, was the religious leader who also played an important role in the Native American Society.

FAMILIES AND VILLAGES

Clans were then divided further into families and villages. They often would play a more important role in their daily life. Larger, extended families would often live together.

Native American Village in Denver, in 1869

RULES AND PUNISHMENT

While punishment would vary from one tribe to another, it typically would not involve any type of physical punishment. If someone committed a crime or went against its tribe, they were generally rebuked and shame in front of their tribe. In more extreme cases, they would be expelled from their tribe.

Native American Tribe

ROLE OF WOMEN

Generally, the women were in charge of the home, and occasionally the fields, which meant they had to work extremely hard.

Native American Woman

* They would cook and prepare the meals. This might involve skinning and cleaning the prey, gathering nuts and fruit, building the fire, and smoking the meat so that it could be stored for the winter months.

* They had many crafting skills which they would use around the house including weaving cloth, preparing animal hides, making baskets and making clothing.

* Many of the tribes held the women responsible for harvesting crops, even though the men would occasionally help.

* The Native American women also had other jobs including gathering firewood and raising the children. When the tribe would relocate, typically it was the job of the women to pack everything up in the house for the move and then once they arrived at the new location they would have to set everything back up.

In many cases, they actually were in charge of gathering the materials and building homes for everyone. They also maintained the roofs. This was an amazing achievement, particularly for women during this time period. The men believed them to be the source of life, and provided the men with a feeling of consistency and strength.

* The Native American women also would often assist the men in hunting down buffalo and once it was harvested, they were still responsible for the skinning, cutting, and the cooking of it.

ROLE OF MEN

The men of the tribes would take care of the activities that occurred away from home.

Native American Man

* Hunting and fishing was the primary job of the men of the tribes. Not only were the animals used for food, but the skins were in making their clothes and, occasionally, in making their homes.

* They were also responsible for making war and protection of the village.

* The typical men's crafts consisted of how they did their jobs such as using weapons for hunting and boats for traveling and fishing.

* Men were the religious and political leaders in most of the Native American tribes. They would also often do heavy work such as planting crops and construction of permanent homes.

WHAT ABOUT THE CHILDREN?

The children had a typical child's life as far as playing, education, and dealing with parents. They were encouraged to make toys and dolls, and express themselves however they saw fit.

Native American Children Going to School

AND THE GRANDPARENTS?

The grandparents would play an important role by teaching the children by storytelling and by teaching them about the Native American lifestyle.

Grandparents telling stories

CHAPTER 2:
Where Do They Live?

Native Americans built and lived in many different types of homes. The different tribes would build different homes, depending on the materials available to them as well as where they were located. Their lifestyle was taken into consideration as well as the environment.

WIGWAM

The homes that were constructed by the Algonquian tribes that lived in the northeast were known as wigwams. They consisted of bark and trees, like the longhouse, however, they were easier to build and were much smaller.

Wigwam

The wigwam was a relatively small home, forming a circle approximately 15 feet wide. However, these homes would sometimes house more than one Native American family. It may have been a tight squeeze, however, it probably kept them warm during the winter.

There would be a flap at the top of it that was opened or closed using a pole.

Wigwam

HOGAN

Constructed by the Navajo peoples of the Southwest, the Hogan consisted of wooden poles used for the frame, which was covered in adobe, a clay mixed with grass. Generally, it was shaped like a dome and the door would face to the east, towards the sunrise. There was a hole at the top to enable smoke from the fire to escape.

The Hogan was often constructed with railroad ties after the 1900s.

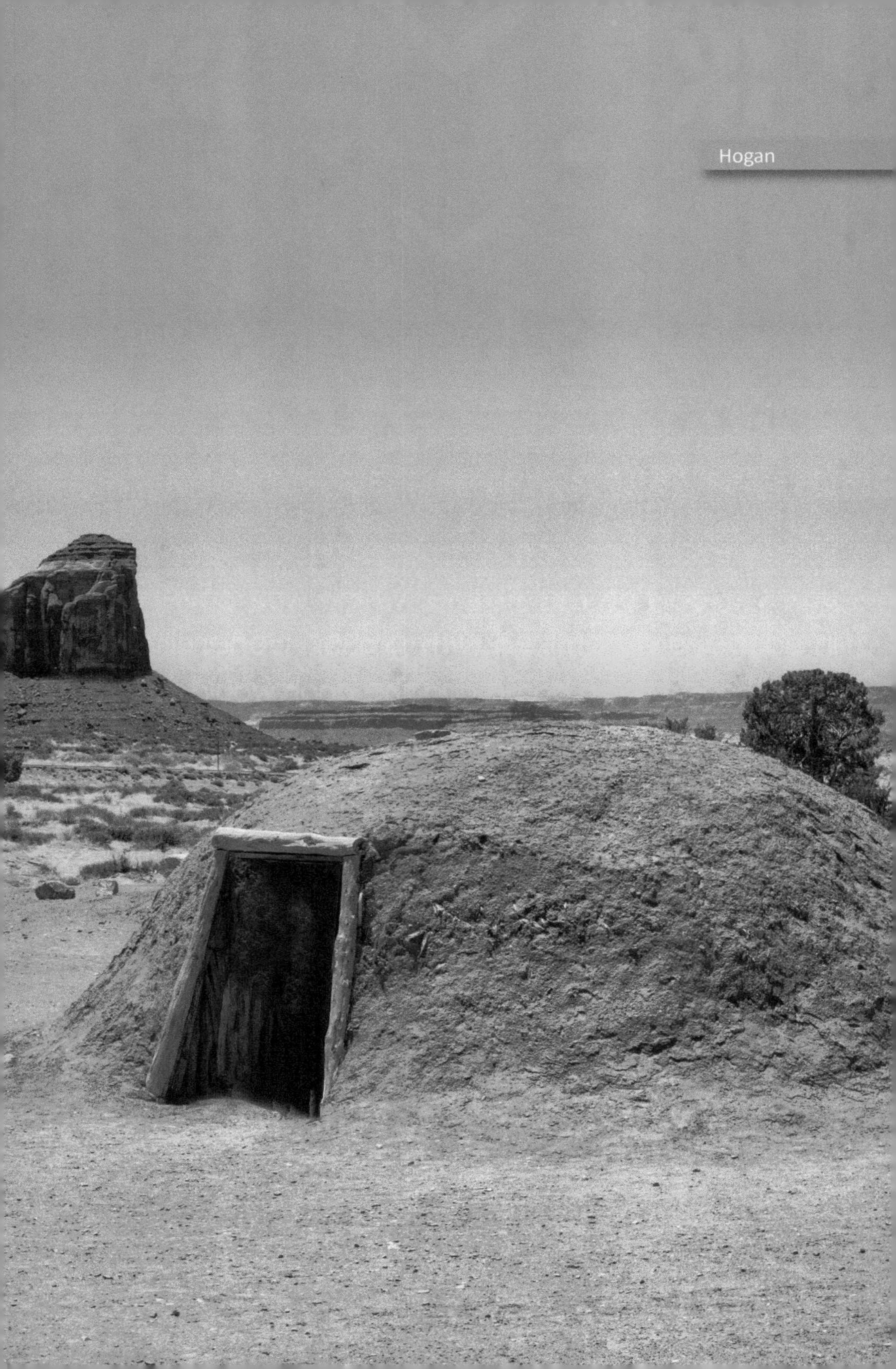

Hogan

TEEPEE

These were the houses for the Great Plains nomadic tribes. They were constructed using several long poles for the frames which were tied together at its top and spread apart at the bottom, creating an upside-down cone shaped home. The outside was then covered with a large piece of buffalo hide.

Typically, the teepees where the medicine men lived were decorated with paintings.

Teepee

NATIVE AMERICAN LONGHOUSE

This home was constructed by the Northeast American Indians, in particular, the Iroquois nation. The Iroquois were also referred to as the Haudenosaunee, meaning "People of the Longhouses".

These permanent homes were built from bark and wood and were constructed in the form of a long rectangle and were approximately 18 feet wide and 80 feet long. This is how they got their name. They had a door at each end and there would be holes in the roof allowing the smoke from the fires to escape.

Native American Longhouse

PUEBLO

The Native American pueblo was built in the Southwest by American Indians, in particular, the Hopi tribe. These shelters were permanent and sometimes a part of bigger villages, housing hundreds, maybe thousands of people. They would often be constructed inside of caves, or sides of larger cliffs.

Pueblo

OTHER TYPES OF NATIVE AMERICAN HOMES

The plank house was built near the coast by natives located in the Northwest and were made from cedar plans. Many families lived in one home.

Plank House (front view)

Plank House (side view)

Igloos were built in Alaska by the Inuit. They were small homes shaped like domes and made of ice blocks. The igloos were able to keep the tribes warm during the cold winters. The fire inside the igloo was created by animal oil in a large dish which was used similar to a candle.

Inuit building an igloo

The chickee was erected by the Seminole tribes and consisted of a thatched roof which kept the rain out, however, the sides were open so they could remain cool during the Florida hot weather.

Chickee

Chickee

The wattle and daub was like the chickee, but used clay and twigs to create walls. It was constructed by tribes located in the northern, somewhat colder areas, like the North Carolina Cherokee.

Wattle and daub construction

Wattle and daub

CHAPTER 3:
What Do They Wear?

Native American clothing was different dependent upon their tribe as well as what climate they lived in. There were, however, some similarities.

Primarily, they would use animal hides to make their clothes. They would typically use hides of the animals they had hunted to eat. Some of the tribes, including the Iroquois and the Cherokee would use deerskin. The plains Indians, known to hunt for bison, would use buffalo skin and the Inuit tribe from Alaska would use caribou or seal skin.

There were a few tribes that learned to make their clothes from plants or by weaving threads. The Navajo, Apache and Seminole tribes of Florida learned to make tunics and blankets.

DECORATIONS

The clothing would often be decorated. They would use animal fur including rabbit or ermine, feathers and porcupine quills. Once the Europeans arrived, they also started using glass beads when decorating their clothes.

Rabbit Skin Blanket

Feather Headdress

Craddle Borad Porcupine Quills

Glass Beads Amulet

HEADDRESS

The feathered type of headdress that you are used to seeing in a book or on television was not the most popular headdress. The more popular type of headdress was called a roach, which was made from the hair of an animal, typically the porcupine hair because of its stiffness.

Native American Indian
Chief Headdress

FOOTWEAR

Most of the Native Americans would wear some type of footwear. It would usually be a shoe made with soft leather called a moccasin. In the colder northern areas such as Alaska, they were a mukluk, which is a thick boot.

Moccasin

Mukluk

WHAT DID THE MEN WEAR?

Mostly, the men would wear a breechcloth. This was simply a piece of material they would tuck in a belt which covered the back and front. In several areas, especially those where the weather was warmer, this would be all that they wore. In the cooler climates, the men wore leggings to keep their legs warm and cover up. Many would go without a shirt for much of the year, only using a cloak if it got too cold. The Plains Indian men were well-known for their decorated and elaborate war shirts.

Breechcloth

Wearing a Cloak

War Shirt

WHAT DID THE WOMEN WEAR?

They would generally wear leggings and skirts. They would also often where tunics and shirts as well. In some of the tribes, like the Apache and the Cherokee, the women would wear a longer buckskin dress.

Tunic

Buckskin Dress

CHAPTER 4:

How Do They Entertain Themselves?

The Native American Indians would enjoy a variety of entertainment in the form of games, sports, festivals, music and dance. The different tribes in different regions would have their own traditions and games.

Traditional dancer at Native American pow-wow

LACROSSE

Lacrosse was one of the most popular sports of the Native American Indians. It is still popular today. The different tribes would have different names for lacrosse which included bump hips, stickball, little brother of war and kabucha.

It was played by passing a ball around using sticks that had nets attached at the end. Often the game would be a huge event with hundreds of players on each side and a field over a mile long. They would often last all day.

There was another version of the game that women would play called amtahcha.

Lacrosse

ACROSSE STICKS AND
SAUK AND FOX

HAND GAME

The Hand Game was a game that was played with two teams. One team would quickly pass a ball or small bone to another teammate. The other team would then attempt a guess as to who had the item. If they would guess right, they would get a point. Then it was the other team's turn to hide the item.

Hand Game

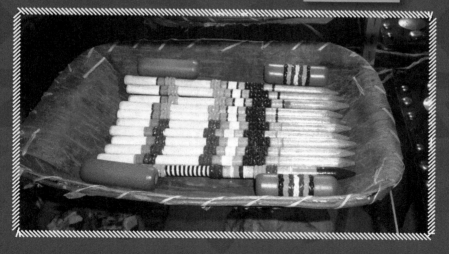

RING-THE-STICK

The Ring-the-Stick game was more of a children's game. They would tie a string on an end of a stick and there would be a ring tied to the other end. They tossed the ring and attempt to catch the ring with the point on the end of stick.

Ring-the-Stick

BOWL GAME

The Iroquois enjoyed the Bowl Game, which traditionally would be played at the Midwinter Festival. A wooden bowl is used with six nuts which were white one side and black on the other side. These nuts would be placed in the bowl. The player would throw the bowl to the ground and when at least five nuts would end up showing the same color, they would gain a point.

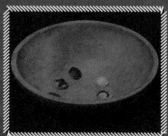

Bowl Game

MUSIC

Dance and music were important to the culture of the Native American peoples. They would sing during important religious rituals, but also as a part of their daily life. They felt that it was the spirits talking to them.

Music

DANCE

There also was a great variety of traditional dances they would perform. Each one would have its own name, songs, steps, meaning and history. Some of them would include both women and men and other ones were for just the men or the women. Many involved the dances performing in a circle. They would sometimes dress up with masks and/or costumes.

Bear Dance

Some examples of dances of each specific tribe include:

* Grass Dance (Sioux) Devil Dance (Apache)

* Bow and Arrow Dance (Navaho)

* Buffalo Dance (Sioux)

* Doll Dance (Navaho)

* Snake Dance (Hopi)

GAMBLING

Gambling became very popular with the Tribes and often the stakes were very high. Players often would even wager a horse or valuable furs.

Gambling

CHAPTER 5:

How Do They Gather Food?

Depending on the area they lived in and the tribe they were a part of, Native Americans would get their food by varying methods that included farming, gathering, fishing and hunting. Most of the tribe would use a combination of these methods to obtain food, however, several would focus on a certain area such as hunting or farming.

FARMING

Several of the American Indian tribes would grow crops for food, however the farming experts would tend to be in the southern states such as the Southwest and Southeast. Tribes such as the Cherokee and the Navajo would grow large crops and utilize advanced procedures like irrigation in order to supply to the dry areas and crop rotation which would keep the ground fertile for several years. They would also grow extra food to store it and be able to survive the winter months.

Farming

GATHERING

When people obtain food from their environment, it is referred to as gathering. The Native American tribes gathered foods including nuts, berries, or other fruits produced from naturally growing berry bushes and trees. Many of the Native American peoples used gathering to obtain some of their food.

Gathering

HUNTING AND FISHING

Several tribes obtained most of their food by hunting, which was a major part of the Native American culture.

Hunting Fish

HUNTING BISONS

In the Great Plains area, they relied greatly on buffalo, also known as bison. They not only ate it for food, but also used much of it for other aspects of their lives. The bones were used for tools. The hides would be used for clothes, blankets, and for making the covers for their teepees. They would make rope from the bison's hair and use their tendons as thread for sewing. Most all parts of the bison were utilized.

Hunting Bisons

The bison is a large and powerful animal that travels in large herds. To be able to hunt them, the American Indians would need to work together and be clever. Often, they would get them to stampede into a pit or off of a cliff.

Hunting Bisons

HUNTING OTHER ANIMALS

The Native American Indians that lived in other parts of the country would hunt using weapons like the bow and arrow or use traps and snares for hunting rabbits, ducks, deer and other such animals.

Hunting Deers

FISHING

Tribes living near large lakes or in coastal areas specialized in fishing. They would often use nets or spears to catch fish, which was smoked or dried and stored for the winter months. Native Americans living in the north would ice fish, by cutting a hole in the ice and the using spears to catch the fish.

Fishing

WHAT WERE SOME TYPICAL NATIVE AMERICAN FOODS?

As discussed early, maize was the most important Native American Indian food crop. Most of their tribes grew some corn, and tribes that didn't would trade for it. Other examples of their crops included squash, beans, pumpkins, wild rice, sunflowers, potatoes, tomatoes, sweet potatoes, peanuts, peppers, papayas, and avocados.

Crops

Most tribes ate meat-heavy diets, whether they farmed or not. Some of their favorites meats included elk, buffalo, rabbit, deer and caribou; salmon and other types of fish; geese, turkeys, ducks and other birds; clams and other species of shellfish; and marine animals such as seals and even whales. Almost any animal was occasionally added to the menu, animals you might not think of eating, such as monkeys, snakes or porcupines.

Woman standing by racks of drying meat

Many tribes had strong beliefs against letting food go to waste, so if an animal was killed for another reason, they would go ahead and try to eat it.

Mandan girls gathering berries

They also enjoyed some foods found naturally including honey, eggs, maple syrup and sugar, nuts (including pine nuts, peanuts, cashews, acorn and hickory nuts), fruit (including strawberries, cranberries, raspberries, blueberries, wild plums, chokecherries and persimmons), as well as a variety of roots, greens and beans.

CHAPTER 6:
What Is Their Art Like?

Every tribe has a unique culture and this is reflected in their art, both past and present. Native American art spans thousands of years of history and includes beautiful beadwork, elaborate silver and turquoise jewelry, basketry and weaving. It also includes pottery, many different types of carvings, as well as kachinas, which are dolls representing spirit beings. Carved masks and the musical instruments of drums, pipes, and flutes were used in their performance art, as were headdresses. Totem poles told their stories and showed their skill with carving wood.

ART MATERIALS

Some of the earliest art created by Native Americans were cave paintings as well as earthenware and works made of stone that date back to thousands of years ago. Over the years, they used rocks and feathers to create art, and then in later periods, they used different types of cloth, glass, and clay. In their jewelry, turquoise and silver combinations have always been popular. Each piece of art reflects the different tribes of native people.

Feathers

Rocks

CAVE PAINTINGS

Archaeologists and art historians believe that Native Americans drew rock paintings as part of their spiritual ceremonies. Preservation is important when these ancient treasures are discovered. The pictures are fragile because they were created in the mud. Mud was all around, especially in the southeast portion of the United States, and made a good canvas on the walls of a prehistoric cave.

In these ancient paintings, human beings are shown participating in ceremonies. Sometimes they are doing something heroic or something they would like to do, such as fly, transform into animals, or reach through rock walls.

A common theme in rock paintings, in addition to human forms, is to depict anthropomorphs. These are either animals or spiritual beings that are shown as humans. For example, a buffalo that was drawn walking like a human would be an anthropomorph. Sometimes anthropomorphs are shown with exaggerated features like huge ears, enormous horns, or large hands with extra-long fingers.

Cave Paintings

SPIRITUALITY AND NATIVE AMERICAN ART

The Native American tribes have a deep spiritual connection with all of nature. The sun and the moon are frequent symbols in their art. Bears and eagles were two types of animals that were frequent subjects. Bears represented strength and courage. Eagles represented peaceful friendships. This deep tie to Mother Nature is apparent in almost all Native American art. Jewelry pendants as well as statues were created in honor of Mother Nature and the bounty she provided. Artists and craftspeople took the time to make even ordinary objects beautiful.

TOTEM POLES

Totem poles are sculptures that are carved from very large trees like the Western Red Cedar. Many of the native peoples in the Pacific Northwest and Alaska created totem poles.

Totem Poles

In addition to being an amazing work of art, a totem pole tells a story or is a visual history of an important event. Each figure that is carved on the totem pole is part of the story or event. A totem records the story or history for future generations to remember. Unlike other cultures who used sculptures mostly to represent their gods, the Native American totem pole generally represents characteristics or traits of the particular tribe or clan of the story that's depicted.

Totem Poles

JEWELRY

Jewelry created by Native American artists is rich with symbolism from nature and their enduring legends. It's used for many reasons. One reason is simply decorative. Another is to protect. A third reason is to honor. A fourth reason was to show the social class of the individual wearing it. Native American jewelry is sought after by collectors for its elaborate designs and intricate patterns. Most of the inspiration for the jewelry comes from the natural world. As well as the commonly used silver and turquoise, one of the other materials used was copper.

Copper was used before the Europeans introduced the Native Americans to silversmithing. They also used gemstones such as opal and onyx. Europeans also introduced glass beads, which the Native Americans used to create new types of beaded jewelry.

Jewelry

THE OJIBWE DREAMCATCHER

A completely unique form of art that was created by Native Americans in the Southwest is the dreamcatcher. The Ojibwe tribe created this interesting form of art that looks something like a net that's hung sideways with adornments of feathers or beads on it. The dreamcatcher has a spiritual meaning. The holes are thought to filter out negative feelings. It was sometimes hung to help children avoid nightmares at night. Dreamcatchers have become very popular and have inspired jewelry designs as well as other art forms.

Ojibwe Dreamcatcher

NAVAJO RUG WEAVING AND SAND PAINTING

The weaving of blankets and rugs is another beautiful form of art in which the Native Americans excel. Women would spend hundreds of hours to make the intricate rainbows of patterns and elaborate designs used in the blankets and rugs. The Navajo have a legend that the Spider Woman created the fabric of the universe and when she was finished, she taught her secrets of weaving to the Navajo tribe. It is a tradition that has been passed down through hundreds of years through the generations.

Sand Painting

We generally think of art forms as something permanent, but the Navajo tribe creates beautiful sand paintings as part of their ceremonies. These are intricate mandalas. A mandala is a geometric figure that has spiritual significance. To the Navajo, each color and design element in their paintings has meaning for the sacred ceremony they will perform to worship their gods. The designs show the Navajo myths. A representation of the underworld appears in the middle with rays coming out from the center that represent the gods.

Navajo Rug Weaving

CHAPTER 7:
What Do They Believe In?

The many Native American tribes of North America had a wide range of beliefs and practices. But there were some beliefs that almost every tribe shared. Here are some:

Native American Beliefs

The Great Spirit

THE GREAT SPIRIT

Native Americans believed that while each person each animal, and every living thing is an individual, it is also connected to all other living things. That connection is through the Great Spirit, a creative force that gives us life and meaning. Some tribes called it the Great Mystery, the puzzle of life that we spend our lives trying to understand. The Great Spirit fills, and is the reason for, everything in the universe, from the stars down to drops of water.

THE IMPORTANCE OF ANIMALS

Spirit Animal

In the story of life for Native Americans, the animals are as filled with the Great Spirit as people are. Sometimes animals speak to people, guide them, or warn them. Some tribes understood a certain animal to be their special protector or "totem", giving members of that tribe special powers or ways of living in the world.

Many tribes thought that each individual animal was an image of the spirit of that species. Every fox was an image of the one Fox, and every bear of the one Bear.

Spirit Animal

THE FOUR DIRECTIONS

The Four Directions are points of balance in the Native American world view. They can be the points of the compass, four animals, or even four colors. Sometimes a fifth point of balance appears in the center of the Four Directions, like four brothers with their sister in the middle.

Four Directions

MYTHS AND LEGENDS

Likes myths around the world, Native American myths and legends include common themes or "archetypes". Here are some:

*   The hero who has to take a journey (Odysseus in the Greek myths; First Woman in the Native American myths)

*   The orphan who becomes a great hero

*   The wise old woman who helps the hero

*   The trickster who must be defeated (Loki in the Norse myths; Coyote in some Native American myths)

THE FLOOD

Many Native American tribes shared a myth of a great flood. In most of the stories, a partly human creature sends a diving bird or a diving animal to get some mud or sand from under the sea to restore the land.

Native American Stories of Great Flood

STAR-BORN

In many myths, the mother or father of the hero is a star, and then the hero comes to live on Earth and lead the people.

Star-born

THE OLD MAN

Many tribes told long stories, with many episodes, of The Old Man, a magical human who could change his shape and who worked to right wrongs and defeat evil, but who also played tricks on people.

Among the Plains Indians and tribes on the Pacific Coast, the same stories appear about Coyote; and some tribes tell the stories about a spider called Unktomi.

Unktomi

WHITE BUFFALO WOMAN

The tribes of the Great Plains have as their central myth the story of how the people received the sacred peace pipe, and learned the ceremony of smoking it. In the myth, White Buffalo Woman appears to the people, gives them a bundle with a pipe and a sacred stone, explains the markings on the pipe and the stone and how and where to use them. Then White Buffalo Woman walks around the teepee where the people are gathered, turns into a white buffalo, and leaves the people. When the people smoke the pipe together, they are also sharing it with the spirit world.

ANIMAL ORIGINS

Many myths try to explain how animals came to be as they are. In one Blackfoot myth, the trickster character is angry and tries to pull the lynx in half, but he only gives it a longer body.

Blackfoot Myth

THE GREAT SPIRIT IN ANIMALS

In many tales and myths, The Great Spirit, or the spirit of the prime animal (Coyote or Wolf, for instance) works through the specific coyote or wolf in the story to help the human characters in some way. In other stories the Great Spirit works through imaginary animals, as when Thunderbird (a creature like an eagle) makes lightning and thunder happen.

The Great Spirit

RELIGIOUS PRACTICES

Native American rituals are closely related to how they traditionally gathered food, and give a way to celebrate and respond to important stages in life, like birth, coming of age, marriage, and death.

Spiritual beliefs and practices

DEATH CEREMONIES

Native Americans believed that death in this world opened the way to life in the Spirit World. Many rituals were to help the dead person find the path and start on the journey. In rituals, people would offer the dead person the food, herbs, and other gifts needed on the journey.

Navajo people believed that if a person died by accident, suicide, or sudden illness, instead of dying of old age, an evil spirit, a "Chindi" could cause trouble for the dead person's family. Rituals lasting several days tried to restore order in the family and in the Spirit World.

Death Ceremonies

GREEN CORN FESTIVALS

People of the eastern woodlands and the southeastern part of North America held celebrations in the late summer to give thanks to the Great Spirit for corn, rain, sun, and the harvest. This is also a time for council meetings at which minor problems and even crimes that took place in the past year could be forgiven. This helped restore the spirit of the community.

Green Corn Dance

HEALING RITUALS

Many different rituals tried to help restore harmony in a sick person, in a troubled family, or in a divided community. Tribes like the Navajo and Sioux would have ceremonies lasting several days, involving burning herbs, sacred dances, sand paintings, story telling, and times of silence.

White Wolf, Ancient Healing

PEYOTE WORSHIP

Tribes in the southwest have often performed ceremonies involving peyote (the fruit of a small cactus) or sacred mushrooms. The tea made from these materials could put the person who drank it into a sort of a waking dream, where the person could perceive reality differently and possibly hear a message from the Great Spirit or other spirits. The ceremonies also involved burning incense or herbs in a fire to help cleanse the mind, and wearing bird feathers to try to gather strength and vision from the bird spirits.

Peyote Ceremony

Peyotism

Flowering Peyote Cactus

VISION QUESTS

For many tribes, young men took a "vision quest" to try to find the direction of their lives. This was part of becoming an adult member of the tribe. The ritual and the quest varied from tribe to tribe, but usually involved a spiritual experience in which the young man tried to connect with a guardian spirit for advice or to gain strength.

Vision Quest

CHAPTER 8:
Native Americans Today

Some descendants of the original American Indians now live on areas of land that is specifically set aside for them, known as reservations. This is to help maintain and protect their culture and heritage, even though only about 30% live on these reservations. The rest of them live just like anyone else does, outside of the reservations.

ENTERING
PINE RIDGE
INDIAN
RESERVATION

THE INDIAN RESERVATION

An area of land that is managed by a tribe under the Bureau of Indian Affairs is known as an Indian Reservation. There are 326 Indian reservations in the U.S. and each of them is associated with a Nation. Not all 526 tribes have a reservation; some tribes might have more than one, some tribes share reservations, and other may have none. Also, due to land allotments in the past, some of the reservations are fragmented, with each piece of individual, tribal, and privately held land being considered a separate enclave. This creates significant political, legal, and administrative difficulties.

Indian Reservations in the Continental United States

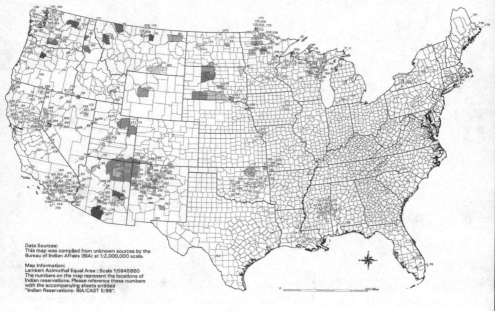

Data Sources:
This map was compiled from unknown sources by the
Bureau of Indian Affairs (BIA) at 1:2,000,000 scale.

Map Information:
Lambert Azimuthal Equal Area ; Scale 1:5845860
The numbers on the map represent the locations of
Indian reservations. Please reference these numbers
with the accompanying sheets entitled
"Indian Reservations- BIA/CAST 5/96".

0 _____ 500 Miles

The term "reservation" stems from the idea that the Native American tribes were independent sovereigns during the time that the Constitution of the United States was ratified. Therefore, early peace treaties, which often were signed under duress, in which the Native American tribes had surrendered portions of land to the United States, also designated areas of land which the tribes reserved for themselves, and they became known as "reservations". This term remained in place even once the government started to forcibly relocated the tribes to parcels which they had no historical connection to.

Most of the Alaska Natives and Native Americans live outside the reservations, often in large cities in the west such as Los Angeles and Phoenix. There were more than 2.5 million Native Americans in 2012, with only approximately 1 million of them living on the reservations.

Alaska Native

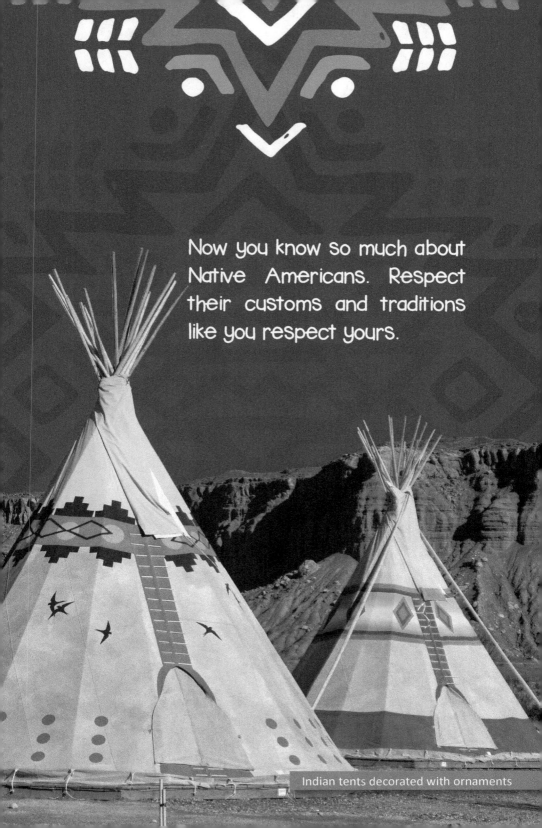

Now you know so much about Native Americans. Respect their customs and traditions like you respect yours.

Indian tents decorated with ornaments

A silhouette of a Native American on a horse